Pierre Elliott Trudeau

The Prime Minister Canadians Either Loved or Hated

by Stan Sauerwein

To Pierre Elliott Trudeau's children,
Justin, Michel, Sacha, and Sarah

PUBLISHED BY ALTITUDE PUBLISHING CANADA LTD.
1500 Railway Avenue, Canmore, Alberta T1W 1P6
www.altitudepublishing.com
www.amazingstories.ca
1-800-957-6888

Based on a book with the same title
by Stan Sauerwein, first published in 2004.

Extreme care has been taken to ensure that all information presented in
this book is accurate and up to date. Neither the author nor the
publisher can be held responsible for any errors.

Publisher	Stephen Hutchings
Associate Publisher	Kara Turner
Junior Edition Series Editor	Linda Aspen-Baxter
Editor	Lisa Lamb
Cover and Layout	Bryan Pezzi

We acknowledge the financial support of the Government
of Canada through the Book Publishing Industry Development
Program (BPIDP) for our publishing activities.

Altitude GreenTree Program
Altitude Publishing will plant twice as many trees as were used
in the manufacturing of this product.

ISBN 10: 1-55439-702-2
ISBN 13: 978-155439-702-0

Amazing Stories® is a registered trademark of Altitude Publishing Canada Ltd.

Printed and bound in Canada by Friesens
2 4 6 8 9 7 5 3 1

MAY 1 5 2008

Contents

Prologue

Arab volunteer soldiers didn't ask questions. They helped the young stranger climb into their truck. Perhaps they helped him because he fit right in. He had a bushy brown beard. He was deeply tanned. He also wore a scarf wrapped around his head. It kept the hot sun off him. Whatever the reason, the young man settled into the group of soldiers on the truck. He was ready to enjoy his 60-kilometre ride from Amman to Jerusalem.

It was May 1948. The hitchhiker was in Palestine. It was a country at war. Travelling without proper papers was risky. The 29-year-old student didn't care. He was pleased to have caught a ride. All he wanted was a chance to see Jerusalem. Seeing the Holy City was worth the danger. The truck crossed the Jordan River and followed the highway through Jericho. He checked the directions he'd been given to a monastery.

He had been told to expect Palestinian Army blockades. None threatened his ride. The truck reached the walls of Jerusalem. He grabbed his pack and jumped from the moving truck. He entered the city.

He was excited. Was he walking the same narrow roads Christ may have walked? Was he touching the same dusty stones Christ may have touched? He was filled with memories of Bible stories. He had gone to school in

Montreal. The Jesuits had been his teachers. They had taught him many stories about Jerusalem and the time of Christ. He wandered through the Old City. He imagined what it had been like when Christ had lived. By the time he found the monastery, he was lost in his thoughts. Then there was the crack of gunshots.

He was caught in Israeli-Arab crossfire near the doors of the monastery. He dove to the ground. So did the scared Arabs and Jews around him. He had to crawl towards the monastery. When he got there, he pounded on the door.

Several hours later, the streets were calm. The young man wanted to explore again. The priest at the monastery told him to be careful. He was right. Just a few moments later, the hitchhiker found himself in the middle of gunfire once more. Instead of diving back to the ground, he ran. He charged through the gunfire carrying his pack like a football. To the Arab soldiers, he looked exactly like a scared enemy fighter with explosives. They pounced.

Allah had given them a gift! Their captive had two passports. They knew he had to be a Jewish spy. However, he had an odd name for a Jew. It was Pierre Elliott Trudeau.

Chapter 1
A Young Boy Discovers His Inner Strength

His flaws were many. But they were glorious. Canadians both hated and adored Pierre Elliott Trudeau.

He was a puzzle to many Canadians. He was a proud French Canadian. He had a vision that united Canada. He believed in the strength of Canadians. With that belief and his French Canadian background, Trudeau helped create a more modern Canada.

Pierre grew up in a household in Quebec. Two languages were spoken in his home. In his world, a question might be asked in one language and answered in another. In his house, Catholic prayers were whispered in French. Dinner-table politics were argued in English.

Pierre's grandfather Joseph was a farmer. He had

come from a family of farmers. Pierre's grandmother, Malvina, was a strong woman. Her own father had been mayor of his village. Her brother had been a doctor. Joseph and Malvina had 13 children, but five died.

His father was one of the survivors. His name was Charles-Emile, or Charlie. He took after his mother's side of the family. When Charlie was still quite young, his father sold the farm. He moved his family to Montreal. He wanted his eight children to get a good education, and they did. Two became lawyers. One became a dentist.

It was in Montreal that Charlie met Grace Elliott. She was the woman who would become his wife. Her family was Scottish and French. She was also Catholic. Her family history dated back to the British Empire Loyalists who had settled in Quebec.

Charlie and Grace were opposites. Charlie was lively and loud. He lived every day with passion. Grace was like her name. She was thoughtful and cultured. Their courtship lasted 10 years. In 1915, they finally married.

Charlie became a lawyer. It was tough to make a good living as a lawyer in Montreal. This was especially so because he was French. Big businesses were mostly run in English. If these businesses needed a lawyer, they went to English-speaking lawyers. Pierre's father Charlie did not like this.

Charlie wanted a chance to prove himself as an equal. He didn't want to be a "second-class" lawyer. He knew it wouldn't make him rich or happy. He changed careers. He had a plan that relied on a new invention, the automobile.

An American had been selling Model T automobiles since 1904. His name was Henry Ford. The $850 autos were everywhere. Charlie knew they would all need gasoline, towing, and repairs. He had an idea to form a club. His club would offer a $10 membership with discounts on those services. He decided to call it the Automobile Owners' Association.

Charlie borrowed money from his friends and from his father-in-law to open his garage. During the start-up period, Grace saved every penny. Charlie fought hard to break into the English-speaking business world. For several years, their future was uncertain. But Charlie and Grace were young and hopeful. They had a new vision for themselves.

Soon, Grace gave birth to her first son. Sadly, he died. Shortly after, Suzette was born. Joseph Philippe Pierre Yves Elliott came along a year later. He was born on October 18, 1919. Two years after that, Charles Elliott (Tip) arrived.

Montreal was a wild city in the 1920s. Mobsters, street gangs, and corrupt politicians often made the front page of the newspapers. Charlie Trudeau seemed a perfect match for the times. He was a curser and a shouter. He would fight with his mechanics if he didn't get his way.

After working a long day in the garage, Charlie

might go over to the Club Saint Denis to drink and play cards. It was a club for French Canadian men. If Charlie drank too much, he showed a darker side. Most of the time, Charlie was fun loving. He enjoyed his lively group of friends.

Business soon picked up. Charlie bought a yellow brick home on rue Durocher. It was a friendly home. Friends came to dinner. There were many parties. Neighbours came from many religions and nationalities. There were Jews, Protestants, Catholics, Irish, Scots, English, and French Canadians. They often joined in with the laughter and the parties at Charlie Trudeau's home.

Nearby was the local Catholic school. Students could learn in English or French. Pierre found himself in the English classroom on his first day of school.

Charlie Trudeau expected Pierre to stand up for himself. On his first day of school, Pierre did just that. His best friend was Gerald O'Connor. He was seated in the second grade row just because he came from an English-speaking family. That upset young Pierre. He could speak English very well. There was only one difference between them. Gerald came from an English-speaking family. Pierre's family was known to be French Canadian.

Pierre liked Gerald. He wanted to sit near his friend. That night, Pierre complained to his father at dinner. Charlie shook his head. He understood.

"It's not fair," Pierre told his father. "I should be in the second grade too."

"Then it's simple. Go see the principal and ask him to put you in the second grade."

"Couldn't *you* ask him, papa?"

"No. It's your problem. Knock on his door and ask him yourself."

The next day, Pierre went to the principal's office. He was barely tall enough to see over the principal's wide desk.

"I want to move to the second grade row," he announced in French. His voice was cracking.

"Do you? Second grade is for children who already speak English. Your papa is French."

"What difference does that make?" Pierre clenched his fists at his sides. "It's not fair! I can talk English just as good," he said, and he switched to English.

The principal corrected Pierre's grammar. He said, "Well."

"Well," Pierre nodded.

"Then move to the other row."

Pierre was amazed. It was done, just like that. He just had to stand up for himself. It was a lesson Pierre never forgot.

Charlie also insisted that his sons be strong. Pierre was shy and small. To please his father, Pierre joined in the roughest games — hockey and lacrosse. He began to exercise outdoors on their tiny lawn. He did so even in the coldest winters. He also took boxing lessons from his father.

Pierre became more coordinated. He grew quick and strong. He developed a lightning-fast right cross. He was still shy. He didn't like to stand out from the crowd. However, he learned to have courage. He never backed down from a dare on his street. His friends depended on him.

Soon, Charlie and Grace were able to buy a summer house in Lac Tremblant. Pierre would dress in deerskin and explore the woods. He imagined he was a *coureur de bois,* an explorer without a map. He loved the rough life in the woods. During the long summer days at the lake, Pierre learned to canoe. He also learned to respect the wilderness. He became strong both inside and out.

Canada entered the Great Depression in the early 1930s. By that time, Charlie owned many service stations. He sold them to Imperial Oil for more than a million dollars. That is about $11.4 million today. The Trudeaus were wealthy when the rest of Canada was not. Work was hard to find. In the Prairies, people faced starvation. Poverty was everywhere on Montreal's streets. People worked long hours for $40 a week.

Charlie invested his money into mining and the Belmont Park amusement complex. He invested in the Montreal Royals baseball club. He also supported promising young boxers. Money did not change Charlie. He spent his money freely. He still loved playing cards with his friends. He still threw parties. Charlie left his first home at rue Durocher. He moved his family and his parties to a new home. It was on an upper-class street at the foot of Mount Royal.

Pierre was happy to change schools. As his family grew richer, Pierre was bothered by their money. At his new school, he played and studied with other rich children. His family's money was not as obvious there as it was on his old street and with his old friends.

His new private school was taught in French. The students were taught to think and to ask questions. They were encouraged to love books and to be the best they could be. It was valuable education for Pierre.

One problem was the bullying. Older students bullied the younger students. Pierre did not stand for it. During lunch one day, an older classmate plopped a banana into Pierre's soup. Pierre returned it right away. The older, louder boy challenged Pierre to a fight after lunch. Pierre agreed. He was used to street fights back home on rue Durocher. This boy was just one more bully.

The two boys scowled at each other all through lunch. Friends egged him on. Pierre kept his cold stare frozen on the older boy. When lunch was over, Pierre walked confidently outside. He wasn't being cocky. He'd just bloodied enough noses in his time.

The older boy stared down at Pierre. Why wasn't he worried? The bigger boy backed off. He let Pierre off with a warning. Years later, Pierre admitted he had been frightened. He learned something that day. "You can win some confrontations just by acting confident."

Pierre faced the bullying at school. He also had to face his own feelings about his family's wealth. As time passed, Pierre felt even more guilt. Was it fair that his father's money could buy him a good education? Back at his old home, his friends had to study at crowded kitchen tables in their tiny houses. He had a quiet bedroom of his own. Was it fair that he could buy any books he needed? His old friends had to borrow books and hurry to read them.

These issues were difficult for Pierre because he really loved learning. He read a lot. He challenged himself with his studies. Did he skip a chapter in a textbook simply because it wouldn't be on a test? Certainly not. It was in the textbook for a reason. He wanted to know why.

At school, Pierre was very happy. He was bright. This helped him overcome his shyness. He spoke a lot in class. He questioned his teachers without fear. The wisecracks he made teased his teachers into debates. Pierre was a child of two languages. He switched between being for English and against it. His teachers began calling him *un catholique protestant* or a catholic protestant. His views never seemed to be completely French or English. He constantly challenged his teachers. He defended his right to freedom of thought.

By 1932, guilt had really eaten away at him. The

sadness of the Depression was everywhere in Montreal. Nearly 30 percent of the population needed government money to live. That was about 250,000 residents, He saw the misery as he went to school.

That summer, his father was taking the whole family to Europe. It would give him a break from feeling so guilty.

Chapter 2
Shaped by Grief

Pierre spent the summer of 1932 in Europe. He was 12 years old. He went with his parents, grandfather, sister Suzette, and brother Tip. They travelled in style. That summer was an amazing experience for Pierre. It fed his desire to travel.

Pierre blended easily into each country he visited. He memorized a bit of each language to talk with people. To Pierre, learning to fit in was a game. He was creative and smart. He spoke with desk clerks to order hotel rooms. He was happy touring the museums and the sights. He was young, so he did not understand what was happening in Europe at the time. Pierre knew nothing about Hitler.

By the time he returned to Montreal, he wanted to learn even more. He studied art, music, philosophy, and literature. Politics held no interest for him yet. He rarely read a newspaper. He didn't listen to the news on a radio. He thought the news was a waste of study time. He still loved sports and took up skiing. For Pierre, life was fun. When he was 15, it all came to a sudden end.

In April 1935, Pierre's father Charlie was visiting the Montreal Royals. They were at their summer baseball training camp in Florida. He developed pneumonia and died there.

When Pierre learned of his father's death, his care-free world came to an end. All his childhood dreams vanished. His dreams of being a sea captain, an explorer, or an astronaut fizzled. His father's death put him at the head of the family. In that time of grief, Pierre's attitude changed forever.

At home, life changed as well. In the three years before his death, Pierre's father had made even more money. He left the family a $3 million dollar fortune. (That would be more than $42 million today.) But he could not leave them his fun-loving spirit. The Trudeau home grew quiet.

Grace began going to her Catholic church. Pierre went with her each morning. When Charlie had been around, there was a great deal of laughter and kissing and hugging. After his father died, things changed. There were no more parties. No friends came to visit. French disappeared from the Trudeau home. English was spoken.

At home, Pierre became quiet. On the streets, he was different. He was a mouthy, angry young man. He picked fights with strangers. Maybe he was trying to be a fighter like his dad. Maybe he was trying to figure out who he was after his father died. Or maybe he wanted to show the world he was his own man.

Pierre didn't want to speak the country French his father had spoken. Instead, he took lessons in classical French. He wanted to master a perfect accent. He played with his name. For a time, he was Pierre-Philippe Trudeau. That changed to Pierre Esprit Trudeau. That changed again to Pierre Elliott-Trudeau.

Pierre struggled to find out who he was. He spoke out against the drinking his father had done. He gave up the team sports his father had loved. Instead, he took part in solo sports like diving and skiing.

After his father's death, Pierre was more willing to accept his place at his new private school. He rarely worried about how his old friends saw his wealth. In fact, he changed his attitude about his wealth. He ran with a cheeky crowd of well-to-do children. They called themselves *les snobs.*

Before his father's death, he had enjoyed debates with his teachers. They had been playful and fun. After his father's death, these debates became disruptions in the classroom. Pierre used his intellect as a weapon. In every debate, it became important for Pierre to have the last word.

Britain and France declared war on Germany on September 3, 1939. Pierre still had a year of school left before graduation. The Declaration of War in Europe affected Canadians. In Quebec, Francophones believed this was a British war. It was none of *their* business. Pierre remembered his father talking of how he and many Quebecers had refused to go to war in earlier years. Pierre was determined not to fight either. But he did enrol in the Canadian Officers' Training Corps (COTC). He also continued with his studies.

The COTC program trained students for officer duties. Pierre had to appear at the armory in Montreal twice a week. There, he learned marching drills. He learned how to handle weapons.

Pierre did this, but he did it with an attitude. During one summer of training, Pierre stood at attention with other young French-Canadian men. Their English cadet sergeant barked out instructions. Seven others in Pierre's group followed the orders. Pierre did not move.

"I said hump those shells now, cadet!" the sergeant ordered. "Get going!"

Pierre didn't move.

"What's the matter with you? Are you deaf?" a cadet captain asked.

"*Je ne comprends pas.*" Pierre said he did not understand.

Another captain shook his head. Then he repeated the order in shaky French.

Pierre pretended to understand. "*Bon. Maintenant je vous comprends,*" he answered. "Remember that here in Canada, we are entitled to be commanded in two languages."

Pierre graduated from school in 1940. Then he studied law like his father. At the Université de Montréal, Pierre fit right in. His schooling had prepared him well for university studies.

The war went on. Pierre was still against military service. William Lyon Mackenzie King was a Liberal. He was seeking election. He made a promise to Canadians. He would not force them into military service. When he was elected prime minister, he went back on his word. Pierre was outraged.

Pierre took part in marches. He went to meetings against **conscription**. He was against being forced to fight. He felt strongly about it. Mackenzie King's government could not force the Canadian people to fight the war in Europe. He kept up this fight for years.

In 1942, he was at an election rally. Pierre went to the microphone and shouted, "There is currently a government which wants to invoke conscription and a people who will never accept it. If we are not a democracy, we should start a revolution without delay. They are asking our people to commit suicide. Citizens of Quebec, don't stand around blubbering. Long live the flag of liberty!"

The people did not revolt over the issue. Pierre was

discouraged. He went back to his studies. He was soon bored at university. He lost his interest in law as a career. Pierre decided law school training in Quebec prepared graduates for a "two-bit life among unthinking people."

Pierre still had his sense of adventure. He fed it in other ways. He went on expeditions. One summer, Pierre and three friends decided to paddle to Hudson Bay. Pierre was about 20 years old at the time. He and his friends travelled the old *voyageur* route. They headed westward in canoes along the Ottawa River. Their trip took them northward. They crossed Lake Timiskaming and paddled on to the Harricana River. They followed it all the way to James Bay.

On another trip, they toured the Gaspé Peninsula on foot. It was wartime. Travelling was full of interesting twists. The government was afraid of invasion. When the sun went down, all lights had to be out in Gaspé villages. Pierre and his friends slept in barns and empty classrooms. They were often accused of being part of a German strike force. Time and time again, they had to prove that they were not.

Pierre loved the craziness of this. He made fun of what he saw. He played jokes. One time, he and a friend found old moth-eaten Franco-Prussian uniforms in an attic. These uniforms had been last worn in 1870. They dressed up in these old uniforms and put on the pointed steel helmets. Pierre still remembered what he had learned in Europe when he was 12. He and his friend rode across the countryside on a motorcycle. As they rode, they shouted phrases in German.

Pierre completed his law degree. He began to work for a downtown Montreal law firm. He did not enjoy it. He was miserable. He felt he had made a mistake in becoming a lawyer. What else could he do? Would he ever figure out what would make him happy?

One day, he was listening to someone recite a poem. The person was reading one of Cyrano de Bergerac's poems. By the last line, Pierre knew that he wanted to be like Cyrano:

> ... to sing, to laugh, to dream,
> To walk in my own way ...
> Free to cock my hat where I choose ...
> To fight or write. To travel any road
> Under the sun or the stars ...
> And if my nature wants that which grows
> Towering to heaven like the mountain pine,
> I'll climb, not high perhaps, but all alone!

Pierre still lived at home even though he was in his twenties. He didn't need to keep his mother company. She had a country girl living in the house as her maid. Her handyman driver, Grenier, had worked for the Trudeaus through four decades. Pierre lived there more because he loved his mother. He treasured his time with her.

Pierre dated, but his mother did not approve of many of the girls. Pierre was not really looking for a girlfriend. He was also concerned with how he looked. He worried about how short and thin he was. He was bothered by his skin. He had terrible acne when he was young. It had left scars. He was also shy. He covered up his worry and shyness by clowning around. He might do a handstand in a crowded room just to gain attention.

At parties, he got into loud arguments, even when he didn't really care about the subject. He was very sarcastic. As a young man, he was also once cruel to his fiancée. At a party he said, "If I had hips like yours, I'd give up cake." He may have been joking, but the two did not get married. Pierre left Montreal.

Chapter 3
Finding a Meaning in Life

In September 1944, Pierre went to Cambridge, Massachusetts. He enrolled at Harvard University. It was a month before his 25th birthday. Pierre was not ready to start his career. He wasn't ready to find a wife and raise a family. He thought he was moving away from his mistake of becoming a lawyer like his father.

"I always regarded regret as a useless emotion," he wrote. "I have never looked back at my mistakes, except to make sure I would not repeat them."

At Harvard, Pierre quickly realized something. He was exposed to different ideas there. The other students knew more about the world than he did. Pierre decided that he wanted to learn more about the world around him. He made a sign for his dorm room. The sign said it all: Pierre Trudeau — Citizen of the World.

Pierre wasn't sure what he wanted for a career. Before he left Montreal, he had asked the advice of André Laurendeau. He was a writer Pierre respected.

Laurendeau gave him advice that made sense. Quebec needed professional people who could advise the people and government about **economics.**

Pierre thought about becoming a teacher someday. He decided to study political economy and government for his Master's degree. Harvard gave him what he wanted. His instructors were excellent. They opened his mind. He learned new theories in economics and political science. His beliefs about individual freedom grew stronger. Pierre prepared himself for a teaching career. At the same time, he was preparing for a political career.

Pierre got his degree from Harvard when he was 27. He still wasn't sure what he wanted to do. If it was teaching, he knew it would have to be at the university level. To do that, he would need more education. He would need a doctorate. He finished his written and oral exams. Then he moved to Paris to continue his studies.

The war was over in Europe. Allied victory had been declared May 8, 1945. The city was still feeling the effects of war when Pierre arrived in Paris. Food and clothing were still rationed. Medicine was hard to come by. So was gasoline.

Pierre went to the École Libre des Sciences

Politiques. It was full of France's rich students. Pierre found that he was more comfortable with the other Canadian students. Most of them were poor.

Pierre had money to spend on food and entertainment. He went to parties. He spent long evenings in street-side cafes and bistros. He argued about politics until dawn. Pierre liked to race along the streets of Paris on his motorcycle.

Pierre found the students of Paris weren't very accepting of French Canadians. The courses weren't as good as Harvard's. At the end of the university year, he decided to leave Paris. He would try the London School of Economics (LSE).

Students at the LSE came from all over the world. Each brought new ideas for Pierre to consider. Pierre admired one of his teachers, Harold Laski. Laski was a powerful speaker. He was also the senior officer in the British Labour Party.

"I wanted to know the roots of power. I wanted to know how governments work and why people obey." Pierre learned a lot at the London School of Economics. Everything he had learned about law, economics, and political thought came together for him there.

Pierre had to write a thesis for his doctorate. He decided to write on the relationship between Christianity and Marxism. These were two popular beliefs of the people in Asia. He settled on India as the country to study. There were many Canadian Catholic missionaries there. They would help him. He would also be able to find Marxists there.

He would go to India. He would backpack and use third-class coaches on trains, on buses, and on cargo boats. Along the way, he would just follow his nose. He'd mix with the people to learn about their lifestyles and habits. His travel bug had come back. Research was a great reason to travel.

In spring 1948, Pierre stuffed his backpack with clothes and journals. He spent the first two months tramping through Eastern Europe. He wanted to test himself as a solo traveller. Crossing some borders meant he had to make false documents. In one country, border guards were not fooled. Pierre spent a day in a jail cell before he was let go.

Pierre's hair was long. He had a bushy beard, a hooked nose, and almond-shaped eyes. He had a look that fit in almost anywhere he went. He reached Turkey at the end of that summer. Pierre had already been to Poland, Czechoslovakia, Austria, Hungary, Yugoslavia, and Bulgaria. He was ready for even more exotic sights.

In Turkey, he decided to visit the new state of Israel. Israel had just declared its independence on May 14, 1948. The land called Palestine lay within the same region. There was armed conflict in Palestine. Pierre needed a visa. Canada did not have an embassy in Turkey. Pierre went to the British Embassy. He was given a British passport to attach to his Canadian one.

He visited Beirut first. Then he walked to Amman. Pierre could feel the excitement there. Pierre wanted to learn the latest news about the conflict. He went to the international press. They were at the Philadelphia Hotel. When he spoke with reporters, he was amazed. They were not interested in taking risks. They covered the war from their hotel rooms.

"We don't have the necessary travel documents," they told him. They also warned him that the roads were blocked by Palestine forces. Travel was too risky.

Pierre did not see the risk. He had travelled without papers before. He thought it was worth the risk to visit Jerusalem, the Holy City. Once he got there, he could call a priest to direct him safely. A priest in Beirut told him how to get to the monastery in Jerusalem.

Pierre sat in a main square in Amman. He sipped on a coffee and thought about his travel plans. There was activity all around him. Arab mothers wailed as their sons got into trucks. They were Arab volunteers. As Pierre watched, he got an idea. He looked like those volunteer soldiers. He was wearing a traditional Arab headdress. It protected him from the desert sun. He ran toward the trucks. He tossed his backpack up and climbed into a truck.

The truck rolled on towards Jerusalem without trouble. At the gates to the Old City, Pierre leapt from the moving truck. He followed his written directions to the monastery. Just as he reached it, bullets between Israeli and Arab fighters rang out. He dropped to the ground. He had to crawl on his belly. He reached safety inside the monastery. There, he visited with the priest until the gunfight was over. He left to keep exploring the Old City. Palestinian soldiers captured him and put him in prison.

Why did he have two passports? This concerned the Arabs. They suspected he was a Jewish spy. They kept him jailed for days. They threatened him with death.

Luck was with Pierre. The priest had seen the arrest. He pleaded with the soldiers to release Pierre. The priest told them that Pierre was only a travelling student. The Arabs took the priest's word. They sent him back to Jordan in a truck.

Pierre arrived back in the Jordan city of Amman. He was placed in jail again. These jailers spoke English. Pierre demanded to see the staff from the British Embassy. They worked hard to help Pierre out. He was scolded for being foolish. Finally, he was released.

Pierre kept travelling. He experienced wars in other countries. He arrived in Pakistan soon after India had split into two countries. The border between India and Pakistan was flooded with refugees. There were civil wars in Afghanistan and Burma when he was there. There were wars and attacks in Indochina and China.

Pierre travelled for a year. He had lots of time to think. What did he want to do with his life? Pierre knew that he was different. Others usually chose a profession.

Then they trained for it. Pierre wanted to understand the world.

He believed in freedom and free will. He believed in the Catholic faith as well. Pierre didn't find out who he was. Instead, he discovered who he was not. He was not a lawyer. He was not a philosopher. Perhaps, he was not a teacher either. If not, who was he?

Five years after leaving Montreal, he returned. He still did not know who he was. He didn't know what he wanted to do with his life.

Chapter 4
Building the Foundation for Power

Before Trudeau left to travel, Maurice Duplessis was Quebec's premier. He was very conservative. His government was the Union Nationale. It had great influence on the lives of everyone in Quebec. His policies separated Quebec from the rest of Canada and the world.

When Trudeau returned to Canada, he was disappointed. Duplessis was still in power. Trudeau had travelled the world. He had seen many nations rebuilding themselves. This had not yet happened in Quebec.

Not long after his return, Pierre met up with Gérard Pelletier. He was a reporter for *Le Devoir*. It was a Montreal newspaper. He was covering a workers' strike in the town of Asbestos. During the winter, workers had complained. They needed better pay. Their working conditions had to improve. The workers had gone on strike. The government tried talking to settle the dispute. That didn't work, so they used force. Police squads came in with clubs. They silenced the workers. This had gone on for four months. Premier Duplessis wanted to end the strike, so he made striking illegal.

Trudeau drove Gérard to Asbestos. Gérard had to find information for stories. Trudeau stayed and travelled along with Gérard. Trudeau was like many people in Quebec. He understood the worker's situation. He knew what they were fighting for.

Trudeau spent three weeks in Asbestos. During that time, he got involved. He went to a church hall meeting of miners. Pierre gave a fiery speech. The workers loved it. They began calling him Saint Joseph because of his bushy beard and lively speech.

From his travels and time at school, Trudeau had developed a strong belief. Democracy was the highest form of government. He also had another belief. **Federalism** was the highest form of democracy. The workers in Asbestos were applying their rights to democracy.

The experience in Asbestos helped Trudeau. He finally came to a decision. He had to teach. He wanted to teach the brightest young minds in Quebec. He wanted to inspire them to believe in democracy. He applied to teach at the Université de Montréal. He could not be hired. Premier Duplessis "didn't want any professors who had studied in a communist environment, in London and in Paris" teaching there.

Trudeau moved to Ottawa to work. He was 30 years old. A friend helped him get a job as a **civil servant**. He would be able to use his law training and French language. In this job, Trudeau would see how the government worked. He worked in this job for two years.

As a French Canadian, he found the job degrading. Civil servants from Quebec were second-class. Trudeau thought the members of Parliament (MPs) from Quebec were also second class. He saw them as "trained donkeys." They worked under the whips of their masters. Their masters were the English Canadians.

By late 1951, he'd had enough. He didn't need to work for the paycheque. He had learned as much as he could. The labour movement offered him work. Pierre took it gladly. He returned to Quebec.

With his new job, he had to travel. Several times a month, he jumped on his motorcycle. He travelled to cities across Quebec. He taught classes at labour action schools. He taught basic economics. He helped resolve disputes between workers and their bosses. The experience helped him learn more about workers and their rights.

Premier Duplessis died in September 1959. An election was called. Jean Lesage won the next election. He became the new Liberal premier of Quebec. There was no longer a rule about hiring. The Université de

Montréal offered Trudeau a position. Pierre joined the law faculty. He became a professor of public law.

Trudeau finally felt he was where he should be. He was happy. Duplessis was gone. The people of Quebec could make changes like he had seen in other countries.

It was the fall of 1961. Trudeau began going to meetings with a group of men. These men wanted change as much as he did. There was René Lévesque. He was a former Radio-Canada broadcaster. Trudeau's friend Gérard Pelletier was there. He was the editor of *La Presse.* André Laurendeau also went to the meetings. He was the editor-in-chief of *Le Devoir.* Lastly, there was Jean Marchand. He was the province's most powerful labour leader.

The group discussed how Quebec might change. At the same time, a new drum started beating. It didn't beat a new song. It beat an old rhythm in the province. It was the march to Quebec **nationalism**.

Quebec entered an urgent phase of change. The people of Quebec wanted a new place in Canada. More people began calling for bilingualism. They wanted French recognized as an official language. They wanted biculturalism. They wanted to be seen as a distinct culture in Canada. They also wanted **autonomy** for Quebec. The chant *"Le Québec aux Québécois"* began to be heard. It meant Quebec for Quebecers. This encouraged the nationalists. They began demanding special status, perhaps even independence. From this, a powerful movement grew. People in this movement wanted Quebec to separate from Canada.

Then something happened to disturb feelings in Quebec. Random bombings began to happen more and more. The **Front de libération du Québec** (FLQ) said they were responsible. They were a terrorist group.

For some time, Trudeau had wondered if his days as a rebel were over. Would rebellion only mean driving his car too fast? Would it only mean growing his hair too long? Quebec wanted to be its own country. Trudeau didn't agree with it. He had a new enemy to fight.

In his eyes, Quebec had just won the fight against the rule of their old premier. They had loosened the church's grip on the province. Now they were letting nationalism drag them down. Pierre thought a separate Quebec was a mistake. A strong Canada with Quebec as an equal partner with the other provinces was the way to go. Pierre wanted to take action of some kind. But how?

In 1963, the Conservative Party was not re-elected. The Conservatives were led by John Diefenbaker. Canadians voted in a Liberal minority government. Lester Pearson was the Liberal leader. He became prime minister.

Trudeau was teaching law at the Université de Montréal, He also worked as an editor of *Cité Libre*. It was a magazine he helped create. His writings appeared in it when Duplessis was premier. In those writings, he shared his opposite political thought. Now he used this magazine in a different way. He shared his ideas about federalism. All provinces had to be equal partners to make Canada strong. He criticized the movement to separate.

He kept his eye on the federal Liberals over the next two years. He watched them run the country without majority power. They worked hard to get Quebec to support them before the next election. They wanted Jean Marchand to join them. He was Quebec's leading labour leader. Marchand was willing to run on one condition. He would run if the party also welcomed Gérard Pelletier. He was the editor of *La Presse*. The party also had to welcome another colleague. This third man was a law professor. He may have been too young for government. He was 45. Marchand didn't think so. His name was Pierre Elliott Trudeau.

"These were the sort of men I was looking for. They were men of quality and standing in Quebec. They were men who inspired both some admiration and some fear," Pearson later wrote.

The prime minister gave his blessing. The Liberal Party accepted Marchand, Pelletier, and Trudeau.

In September "The Three Wise Men" called a press conference. It was held at the Windsor Hotel in Montreal. They announced they would run for Parliament. On November 8, 1965, each of them was elected.

Trudeau was visiting London early the next January. He received a call from the prime minister's office. Pearson was impressed with him. He wanted Trudeau as his parliamentary secretary. Pierre tried to duck. He told Pearson he wanted to go to Ottawa to present his ideas. He didn't want to seek power. He thought he needed time as an MP to do his "homework." He told the same thing to Marchand.

Marchand told Trudeau to "grow up … You said you wanted action! This is your chance."

Trudeau accepted the job. He became parliamentary secretary. He kept a low profile. He liked to live quietly in a suite at the Château Laurier hotel. He had fun on weekends, and only in Montreal.

Until 1966, Trudeau quietly learned about parliament. He did his job as parliamentary secretary. He had no major problems. That June, Daniel Johnson became Quebec's new premier. Johnson wanted complete independence for Quebec. He let Ottawa know how much he wanted it. He began to seek the support of Charles de Gaulle. He was president of France.

In Ottawa, Prime Minister Pearson was getting nervous. Pearson watched Johnson closely. Then Pearson and the Liberals set up a committee. Its job was to look at Canada's relations with Paris. Then it was to look at Canada's relations with Africa's French states. Trudeau was made chairman of this committee. By 1967, Trudeau had gone to international meetings in Paris and Africa.

Prime Minister Pearson was impressed.

It had been only 16 months since Trudeau had become parliamentary secretary. Pearson rewarded him again. In April 1967, Trudeau became the minister of justice for Canada.

His friends were happy for him. His enemies were not. John Diefenbaker was the Conservative opposition leader. He was quick to point out Trudeau's rough edges. He criticized the clothes Trudeau sometimes wore to the House of Commons. How could he wear leather sandals, slacks, and a sports coat? How could this egghead be so great? Diefenbaker saw only one side of Trudeau. From an early age, Trudeau had learned he had many sides.

As minister of justice, Trudeau had a new challenge. He met it with gusto. He worked hard. So did Quebec Premier Daniel Johnson. Johnson had invited France's president to Quebec. De Gaulle was to make an official centennial visit to Ottawa. Johnson wanted de Gaulle to come to Quebec before that visit to Ottawa. De Gaulle accepted. On July 23, he sailed up the St. Lawrence to Quebec City. He was on board his cruiser, the *Colbert*. The next day de Gaulle rode in a parade to Montreal.

French Canadians filled the streets of Montreal. They cheered de Gaulle's arrival. At noon, he walked onto the steps of Montreal City Hall. He made a speech to the thousands gathered there. He spoke of the spirit of freedom in France after World War II. He spoke of the affection that modern France held for "the French of

Canada." Then he raised his arms. He made the gesture of the victory "V" with his fingers.

"*Vive Montréal,*" he said slowly.

The crowd roared.

"*Vive le Québec,*" he said more loudly. Long live Montreal. Long live Quebec. Finally, he turned to look at the crowd. He shouted. "*Vive le Québec … libre!*" Long live Quebec … free!

The crowd went wild. Those words would give him a place forever in Canadian history. It was an important moment in Quebec.

They were only four words, but they split Canada on the subject of Confederation. De Gaulle's four words caused many to hear what Trudeau was saying. They heard his call to federalism. Many began to listen to Trudeau, not only in English-speaking Canada. Many began to listen in Quebec as well.

Chapter 5
Trudeaumania

The year 1967 was one of celebration. It was the Centennial, Canada's 100th birthday. Canada also hosted Expo 67. Canadians felt great pride in their country that year.

A year later, Lester Pearson made a decision. He would retire from politics.

Just before that, Trudeau shared his Omnibus Bill. This bill updated Canadian divorce law. It also changed the Criminal Code. It relaxed laws against abortion and homosexuality. Trudeau had to convince the other members of the Cabinet. It was a tough job. They finally caved in.

"Well," the other ministers decided, "if you want to risk destroying yourself, it's up to you."

Trudeau told them he would take the gamble. He

felt Canadians were ready for more relaxed views on marriage and sex. On a national TV program, Trudeau explained his bill. He said, "the State has no place in the bedrooms of the nation". This phrase was taken from an editorial in the *Globe and Mail* newspaper. It had been written by Martin O'Malley. It rang bells for Canadians. In the House of Commons, it sparked fierce debate. The Omnibus Bill became law that month anyway.

Trudeau handled the situation with logic. He kept a cool head. That impressed Pearson. He was convinced the next leader of the Liberals had to be French Canadian. This would have to happen if the Party was to stay in power. He offered his support to Trudeau. He wanted Trudeau to think about running as the Liberal leader.

Trudeau was alarmed at the idea. He did not want to give up any more of his own personal freedom. As minister of justice, he had already given up a huge chunk of his private life. "You no longer belong to yourself," he said. He didn't think he should seek the highest office in the land. He was just a new MP. He had barely been in Parliament for two and a half years. He had only been in Cabinet for nine months.

Pearson pressed further. So did Trudeau's closest friends. They finally convinced him. He had nothing to lose. If he lost, he'd still be an MP. If he won, he could create a new vision of Canadian politics. He could try his ideas on federalism.

On February 16, 1968, Pierre Elliot Trudeau walked across the front lawn from the House of Commons. He went to the National Press Club and declared himself.

The election campaign kept Trudeau busy. He also had to keep working as minister of justice. As minister, he was already crisscrossing the country to every provincial capital. His face was in the news almost daily. He used every chance to promote himself.

He was charming. Once, he pretended to fall down a flight of stairs. Then he bounced up like an acrobat. He looked Canada in the eye and said, "I like to get fun out of life."

Voters had been used to one image of leaders in the past. They had been grandfatherly types. Trudeau was the opposite. Here was a vital man. He was also quite young compared to others. And he had a sense of humour. People could identify with him. Women adored him.

The nation watched Trudeau. He kept appearing front and centre. The nation was gripped with curiosity.

Members of the Liberal party adored Trudeau. They wanted to be near him. They wanted to touch him. Television cameramen and newspaper photographers wanted to take pictures of him. Reporters wrote glowing articles about him.

Trudeau's popularity was like a tidal wave. Older leaders were drowned in it. They were puzzled. What was his secret? He knew nothing of politics. How could he get so much support? The answer was simple. Canadians liked his newness. They liked his pureness. Trudeau won the election.

The nation waited. What would the future be like with their new prime minister? Trudeau was nowhere to be seen. The leadership campaign had been tiring. Trudeau decided to take a vacation. He disappeared. He took his friend Jean Marchand away for a two-week holiday. Trudeau did things his way. If Canadians didn't realize that, they should have.

When Trudeau returned to Ottawa, he moved into his new home at 24 Sussex Drive. This was the first house of his own. Up to that time, Trudeau had lived like a vagabond. While in Montreal, he stayed with his mother. When travelling, he had stayed in student apartments or tiny rooms in the YMCA. As an MP, he had lived at the Château Laurier hotel. He moved into his new home with no more than a suitcase. He didn't know if his stay would be weeks, months, or years.

Trudeau continued to be popular. While Pearson was prime minister, only 15 people were needed to handle his mail. Trudeau's mail was four times that amount. He soon had 60 people on his staff.

There was a question in the prime minister's mind. Should he continue to govern with a minority government? Should he give the Canadian people time to get to know him? Or, should he call an election while he was still hot news? Trudeau asked the Liberal **caucus** for advice. He also asked his friends. They told him to call an election. On June 25, Canada would go to the polls.

The election campaign was a replay of his leadership battle. The adoration for Trudeau returned right away. The press called it "Trudeaumania." Trudeau had seen the need to run for the leadership. He had to fight the evil of Quebec separatism.

He went to the people. He told them it was time justice was done in Canada. Twenty-seven percent of Canadians spoke French. That had to be recognized. It was only just. The neediest Canadians had to be cared for by all Canadians. It was only just.

Trudeau summed up his idea for Canadians in his speeches. He called for a "just society." Trudeau wanted a society that gave equal opportunity to all Canadians. He wanted Canadians to help out those who were most in need.

He reached across the country with unending energy. He spoke to crowds of thousands. They chanted his name. He had pictures taken doing jack-knife dives into swimming pools and back flips on trampolines. Happily, he kissed every girl in sight on the campaign trail. (Trudeau always hated kissing babies.) Canadians liked his sparkling energy.

Once, Trudeau was to appear in Victoria, British Columbia. He had to be lowered by helicopter. Adoring fans had surrounded the hill where he was to speak.

Trudeau had a talent for debate. He had a great memory, and he was very smart. He didn't like making speeches. Trudeau preferred to face small groups or to chat with voters.

Trudeau was very popular in English-speaking Canada. What was happening in Quebec? The separatist movement was strong. Some separatists accused him of selling out their dreams of nationhood. The battle lines between them came to a head on June 28. It was the night before the election.

Saint-Jean-Baptiste Day is a celebration across Quebec. It's a day of parades and parties. It honours French-Canadian heritage. That month, Montreal Mayor Jean Drapeau had invited Trudeau to take part. Then Drapeau changed his mind. He feared separatists would demonstrate. He asked Trudeau to cancel his visit.

The prime minister refused. "If you didn't want me to come, you shouldn't have invited me," he told the mayor. "I've accepted. I'm certainly not going to admit, by backing down, that the prime minister of Canada can't watch the festival of Saint-Jean in his own home town! I've been watching this parade since I was six years old."

Trudeau arrived just as he said he would. He stood on the platform for dignitaries. It was in front of Montreal's city library. For a time, everyone enjoyed the celebrations. Then a group of protesters began to wind their way through the parade. They were members of the

Rassemblement pour l'indépendance nationale (RIN).

Then they started running toward the platform. They threw rocks and bottles. The prime minister was not the only target. The others panicked and rose to leave. Trudeau did not move. The Royal Canadian Mounted Police (RCMP) urged him to go. Trudeau refused to flee.

Television cameras were there. They captured the moment on film. Canadians watched the man they adored. He faced the protestors alone.

"I had absolutely no desire to give in to such a ridiculous display of violence," he said. "I detest violence."

The "night of stones" showed Canada that Trudeau was a man of courage. He was stubborn, and perhaps even foolhardy. In the face of danger, the prime minister was unlike any prime minister before him.

The next day, the nation voted. The Liberals won a majority. They won 155 seats out of the 264 in the House of Commons. Minority governments had been in place in Canada since 1962. Trudeau put an end to them.

Chapter 6
Just Watch Me

T rudeau wanted Parliament to do its work well. He changed the way it was organized. He changed how Cabinet did business. Before, Cabinet meetings had been long and full of arguments. They met several times each week. Sessions could drag on long past midnight. Sometimes, they even met on Sundays. It was not a good use of time.

Trudeau wanted to know what was happening in every ministry. First, his ministers had to know the day-to-day business of their ministries. It was the first time in Canadian history.

Trudeau had been a minister. He knew this would cause more work. But he stuck to his guns. The results were clear right away.

Cabinet met only on Thursdays. It rarely sat for

longer than four hours. Trudeau wanted to begin making the changes he had promised. For this to happen, his Cabinet had to be organized.

By October, Trudeau had created an Official Languages Act. This act recognized that Canada had two languages. Both languages were equal before the law. The act would help heal the divide between English-speaking and French-speaking Canadians.

Trudeau began to place Quebecers in government offices in Ottawa. Before, the language of French Canadians was not given equal treatment. The language of English Canadians had been the language of government. Suppose a Francophone civil servant wanted to write to another Francophone civil servant in Ottawa. The writing had to be done in English. Tours of Parliament were done only in English. This situation could not be accepted for long. Trudeau dreamed of a just society where both languages were equal.

The Official Languages Act was not the only change Trudeau made. His first term in office was busy. Trudeau introduced the metric system. He also introduced a change to elections. Any person or group could donate money to support a candidate. Trudeau insisted they make themselves known. Before, special interest groups could donate money to candidates secretly. In return for their donation, they wanted their special needs met first. With the change made by Trudeau, these groups had to be named. No longer would their needs be met before the needs of Canadians.

Diefenbaker was a former prime minister. He had fixed the Canadian dollar's value against the American dollar. The value was held at 92.5 cents. This made sure that Canadian businesses could compete with American businesses. Trudeau freed the dollar to float with other world currencies. Sometimes the Canadian dollar would be stronger. Sometimes it would be weaker.

Trudeau also created a task force. It had to review each part in the **British North America Act**. It was the first step in a plan Trudeau had. He wanted to bring Canada's Constitution home from Great Britain.

Trudeau wanted to see change happen quickly. He didn't know how long he would be in office. Trudeau became impatient with anything or anyone who slowed him down. He was annoyed by anyone who didn't understand his vision.

Voters had given the Liberals lots of power. This power was going to Trudeau's head. His ego seemed to be growing larger. He appeared self-important. If reporters in the press disagreed with him, he insulted them.

In the House of Commons, there was a change in Trudeau. He went from fun-loving to dreary. He had little respect for most Conservative MPs. He never put down anyone's character. However, he put them down as a group.

Once, Trudeau tried to close up business for a holiday. The Conservatives formed the Opposition. They wanted the House to stay open. Trudeau mocked them. He called them "nobodies." "When they get home, when they get out of Parliament, when they are 50 yards from Parliament Hill, they are no longer honorable members. They are just nobodies, Mr. Speaker," Trudeau replied.

Trudeau had called the media a "crummy lot." They were delighted to get back at him. They put the quote in bold headlines. It was seen by people across the country. Trudeau's staff responded. They asked the nation to give him a break. Remaking Canada is a big job, they said. He has a lot on his mind. Canada didn't have to be told. It already knew.

Quebec was still being difficult. René Lévesque led those who wanted independence for Quebec. Trudeau was fighting for a strong, united Canada. Lévesque wanted to break away from Canada. Lévesque argued that Quebec had to become a nation-state. Then they would deal with the rest of Canada in certain areas of common interest.

Trudeau had battled Quebec nationalism for a long time. He had argued against it since Duplessis was premier. "I entered politics with my friends to prove that French Canadians are as good as anyone else," he said. He believed that French Canadians did not need special status. Trudeau did not believe in a two-nations theory.

* * *

The FLQ was a group of extreme separatists. They wanted Quebec to be an independent nation. They kept using violence to prove their point. By 1969, they had carried out more than 200 violent crimes. Of those, 60 were bombings. There were more bombings that year than in the five previous years combined. One blast at the Montreal Stock Exchange had injured 27 people.

Trudeau responded. He created a new committee. They had to figure out the problems of public security. The FLQ was at the top of their list. He asked the RCMP to gather information on the separatist movement in Quebec.

Trudeau had two things in mind when he made that request. He wanted to know more about terrorist activity. He also wanted the RCMP to know more about separatism. He wanted them to find out why terrorists wanted the break-up of Canada. They wanted a violent separation in Quebec. They could come from good, middle-class families. He wanted the RCMP to understand that.

Trudeau had not meant for the RCMP to investigate legal political parties. But he didn't make that clear. The RCMP began to search for more than bombings. They began to look for more than bank robberies used to finance FLQ violence. Their interest went deeper. The **Parti Québécois** became their target. They searched for the evil of terrorism in everything it did. They were suspicious of writers and the press.

Trudeau's request had not been exact. Because of that, he broke the trust of the Canadian people. The RCMP believed they had been asked to spy on their own citizens.

The fallout came in October 1970. By then, 23 members of the FLQ were in jail. Four were convicted for murders. On February 26, 1971, the police arrested two men who were driving a panel truck. Inside was a sawed-off shotgun. There was also a message announcing the kidnap of the Israeli consul. One of the men was Jacques Lanctôt.

In June, police raided a home north of Montreal. There, the police discovered 136 kilograms of dynamite, ammunition, and detonators. They also found the draft of a ransom note. On that note were plans for the kidnapping of the United States consul.

The Quebec nationalism issue was very hot. The FLQ terrorists had warned of more bombings. A report was collected at the Université de Montréal in the mid-1960s. It claimed that 38 percent of that city's residents lived in poverty or hardship. They wanted change.

On October 5, 1970, James Cross was kidnapped from his home by the FLQ. Cross was the British trade commissioner in Montreal. His captors made these demands:

• Twenty-three "political prisoners" were to be released.

- They wanted $500,000 in gold.
- They wanted their plans broadcast on the radio and published in newspapers.
- People had given police information about terrorist activities. The FLQ wanted those names made public.
- They wanted an aircraft to take them to Cuba or Algeria.
- All police search activities were to stop.
- The Lapalm truck drivers were to be rehired. They had lost their jobs when their company lost its contract with the post office.

The Lapalm truckers had gone to Ottawa to protest their lost jobs. Trudeau had no sympathy. He told them, "*Mange de la merde.*" When translated, it meant "eat shit."

Nothing like this kidnapping had ever happened before. It was called the October Crisis.

"The sheer senseless of it caught us off guard," Trudeau said. "That meant we were badly equipped to deal with it."

Within two days, 30 people were arrested in police raids. Canada was responsible for the safety of James Cross. Trudeau would not "give them [the FLQ] an inch." The RCMP had to investigate. The cabinet tried to buy time. Trudeau allowed one of the FLQ's demands on October 8, 1970. Their plans were read over the CBC's Radio-Canada.

It was less than a week after Cross disappeared.

The FLQ struck again. On October 10, Pierre Laporte was kidnapped. He was the vice premier of Quebec and minister of labour. The crime took place in broad daylight. Laporte was taken from the front of his home.

Within hours, Quebec premier Bourassa called Trudeau. "Pierre, you are going to have to send in the army. You should think about using the **War Measures Act**."

Bourassa was concerned. Angry crowds were gathering in Montreal. They were shouting "*Vive le FLQ*," Long live the FLQ. Bourassa feared a rebellion.

Trudeau showed that he was a calm leader. If he used the War Measures Act, all public freedoms would be suspended. It would mean a state of emergency. "The consequences of such a measure would be extremely serious. We have no proof that it is necessary. I prefer not to think about it," the prime minister said. He did agree to send the army if the provincial government made a formal request. The RCMP kept him informed hourly.

Soon Premier Bourassa received a letter. It had been written by Laporte. He pleaded for his life. The Quebec Cabinet tried to talk with the terrorists. Those talks quickly broke down.

Trudeau decided he had to protect the House of Commons. He ordered the army to guard Ottawa on October 12. Reporters questioned him on the steps of the Legislature the next day. He said that society must take every means to defend itself against a group that was willing to disobey the government.

Tim Ralfe of the CBC asked, "Just how far would you go?"

Trudeau's answer is one Canadians would never forget. "Just watch me."

On October 14, Trudeau called a special Cabinet meeting. What should they do about the kidnappings and the FLQ's demands? The situation in Quebec was spinning out of control.

The following day, a group of respected leaders in Quebec met. René Lévesque was there. He was head of the Parti Québécois. Claude Ryan, the editor of the paper *Le Devoir,* and 14 others also attended. They called for the Quebec government to talk with the terrorists.

Quebec premier Bourassa had a different plan. He presented it to the Quebec National Assembly. He wanted to use the National Defense Act to call on the services of the army. His government supported him. So did all three opposition parties. In total, 7,500 troops were quickly sent to Montreal and Quebec City. (This number included those already in Ottawa.)

It was the early morning of October 16. Bourassa made an official request to Ottawa. He asked them to declare a state of **apprehended insurrection**. He wanted Ottawa to impose **martial law**. This would allow the army to take over justice in Quebec. Trudeau knew he could wait no longer. He imposed the War Measures

Act at 4 a.m. It was the only time the War Measures Act had been enforced in peacetime. (It had been imposed before during the two world wars.)

As a boy, he had stared down street toughs on rue Durocher. He had faced flying bottles and stones in Montreal. Trudeau was ready for a fight again. Within hours, the army and police swooped across the province. They arrested more than 250 Quebec residents. They arrested those who were suspected of being communist or FLQ supporters. They were held for questioning without charges or trial.

Before the arrests were over, 247 more people were taken. These included labour leaders and members of the Parti Québécois. Entertainers and writers were also arrested. Many were held for days. They could not contact a lawyer. They were questioned in ways that were not acceptable. There were many arrests. Only 62 were charged.

The FLQ responded. On October 17, they made an announcement. They had killed Pierre Laporte. They told the police where they could find his body. It was in the trunk of a car. The car had been left near Saint-Hubert Airport. This airport was a few kilometers from Montreal.

The police recovered Laporte's body. He had been strangled by the gold chain of his own crucifix.

Trudeau was deeply saddened. He called Laporte's death "inhuman cruelty."

Trudeau spoke out about the number of innocent people who had been arrested. "Naturally, I would prefer that it hadn't taken place, that the FLQ had never seen the light of day, and that Pierre Laporte were still among us. But wishes do not change reality." Most of Canada agreed with him.

Right after Laporte's murder, the Chenier cell of the FLQ spoke out again. James Cross would also be murdered if their demands were not met. If the "fascist police" discovered where they were, Cross would also be killed.

It took three tense weeks. Canadian soldiers patrolled Quebec streets. Finally, a police raid uncovered the Chenier cell's hiding place. Three FLQ members escaped. Bernard Lortie was arrested once again. He was charged with the kidnapping and murder of Laporte.

Lortie's capture did not stop the actions of the Liberation cell of the FLQ. The clock kept ticking. The police were unable to find James Cross. They did a house-to-house search. Time ticked by. Police finally crumpled.

The police used their last resort. They talked with the kidnappers. They did not want to, but there was no other way. They felt they had to before Cross was also killed. On December 3, James Cross was released. It was 60 days since he'd been kidnapped.

At the same time, five terrorist members were given

a safe airplane to fly to Cuba. One of them was Jacques Lanctôt. All five were later found living in Paris, France.

Two days after Christmas, the last three members of the Chenier cell were captured. Police had found them hiding in a six-metre tunnel. Paul Rose, Jacques Rose, and Francis Simard were all charged. Paul Rose was the leader.

On March 31, 1971, Paul Rose and Simard were sentenced. They were given life sentences for the murder of Pierre Laporte. Bernard Lortie received a 20-year jail sentence for kidnapping. Paul Rose was granted full parole on December 20, 1982. It was proven that he was not there when Laporte was murdered. Jacques Rose was found not guilty of the murder and kidnapping. Later, he was found guilty of taking part after the murder. He was sentenced to eight years in jail. He was paroled in July 1978.

Over the years, all of the terrorists came back to Canada. They went to trial. They were convicted of kidnapping. In July 1980, a sixth arrest was made for the Cross kidnapping. It was Nigel Barry Hamer. He pleaded guilty.

After Cross was released, Trudeau slowly began to relax. The crisis weeks had changed him. They had made him stronger. He knew more than ever what Canada needed. It needed a leader with a firm hand. That leader had to set a course and never hesitate. Canada needed a leader that did not try to do everything at once. Canada's leader had to move along slowly, step by step. This leader had to solve problems with careful thought.

Quebec separatism was still a threat. It was like a disease waiting to grow. Trudeau thought he knew how to solve the Quebec question. It was just a matter of getting there.

Chapter 7
Enter the Flower Child

She was 19 years old. He was 48. He was more than twice her age. It didn't matter much to him or her. Under the hot South Pacific sun, friendships are easy to make. That's how it was for them in December 1967. They met on the island of Tahiti.

Trudeau had been asked to run for leader of the Liberal party. He needed time to decide. He was taking time to relax and think at a tropical resort. He was showing off his water-skiing skills. When he returned to shore, Margaret praised him. She rarely had trouble talking with strangers. Men noticed her warm smile and good looks. That included Pierre. He liked flirting as much as the next man.

They relaxed by the water and talked. Margaret wasn't that excited by Pierre. He was old enough to be her father. But his attitude was young. That interested her. He asked her to go deep-sea fishing a few days later. She agreed to join him.

They chatted for three hours. Then, Margaret wandered over to where her mother was sitting. She had been watching the two of them. She was almost the same age as the man Margaret had met. Her mother was Kathleen Sinclair. She was wife of James Sinclair. He had been the Liberal fisheries minister in the Louis St. Laurent government. She knew about the people in politics.

Kathleen asked if Margaret realized with whom she'd been speaking.

"Oh, Pierre someone or other," Margaret replied.

Not just any Pierre, her mother told her. That Pierre was the minister of justice. It didn't impress Margaret. The truth made her less interested. She decided to blow off their fishing date. "I was young and romantic. Pierre struck me as very old and very square," remembered Margaret.

Trudeau met Margaret again in 1968. They were both at the Liberal Convention. A year later, he tried for a date in her hometown of Vancouver. He had dated other women. He went out with singer Barbra Streisand and Canadian actress Margot Kidder. Still, he hadn't forgotten Margaret.

It had been 18 months since he'd seen her last. In that time, Margaret had graduated. She had gained some new experiences in travel. Margaret was a bit of a free spirit. Her attitude towards men had changed. She realized he was the most powerful man in Canada. She knew women across the country adored him. A passionate romance quickly grew between the two.

Margaret's background was like Trudeau's mother Grace. They were both Scottish. Margaret was young and beautiful. She was witty and fun to be with. She loved dancing, poetry, and Pierre. Pierre was 50 years old. He loved being with a girl so much younger than he was. It was different than what others thought he should do. The two of them dated in secret. Her father's contacts helped her get a six-month job in Ottawa. The couple were able to see each other a lot.

He talked to his friends about Margaret. He thought he was in love with her. He decided to introduce Margaret to his dying mother. That said a lot to Pierre's friends. He was serious about Margaret. Trudeau asked Margaret to marry him. She agreed. Then she returned to Vancouver to become a Catholic.

On March 4, 1971, Canada was introduced to the new Mrs. Trudeau. Pierre and Margaret were married in a small private wedding in Vancouver. Margaret had made her own wedding gown. She was stunning. Only a few photographs were allowed to be taken. The couple was pictured taking their vows. Pictures were also taken of them cutting the wedding cake she had baked. Canadians enjoyed each photo.

Margaret Sinclair Trudeau

Overnight, Margaret became a national celebrity. She was 23 years old. Margaret loved it. The marriage seemed a fairy tale come true. Their first child was born on Christmas Day, 1971. They named him Justin. It was the first child born to a sitting Canadian prime minister in 102 years. On the outside, Margaret looked like she was still living the honeymoon.

Trudeau's relationship with the Canadian people was changing. Canada's economy had been growing since 1962. It was still growing when he took over the prime minister's office, By 1972, things were changing.

Canada had depended on the United States. It was time for Canada to take ownership of their economy. Canada had to protect its culture. It had to expand Canada's trade abroad. Canadian businesses were fearful. They worried that the Americans would not like it. But Trudeau truly believed Canada had to act. Canada had to look after its own interests and well-being.

Across Canada, ordinary citizens were concerned about unemployment and **inflation**. People said their prime minister didn't care. The nation was grumbling. Still, Trudeau pushed through more changes.

The Liberals set up the Canada Development Corporation. Its job was to help build a larger Canadian role in the nation's key industries. They formed Canada's first Ministry of Environment. Then, with Ontario, they cleaned up Lake Erie. The Liberals introduced maternity benefits through unemployment insurance. They voted in a capital gains tax. They also created a youth employment program.

Not everyone liked Trudeau's changes. Some thought they were not enough. But Trudeau felt good about his government's work. He called an election for

October 1972. This time he decided to run the election based on his work not his popularity. He thought Canadians should vote with their heads. But Canadians vote with their hearts first.

On October 22, the Liberals lost their majority government. They squeaked into power. They had only a two-seat edge over the Conservatives.

For the next 20 months, Trudeau led a minority government. He walked a tightrope. His government still managed to introduce new social policy. He wanted to improve the lives of Canada's poor.

In 1974, Trudeau had had enough. He was tired of running the country with a minority government. He forced another election. When the Liberals went to the voters in 1974, inflation was high. So was unemployment.

Experts had no experience with this. How should they deal with the problem of inflation and unemployment rising at the same time? A fix for inflation would cause more unemployment. A new term was coined — stagflation. Stagflation describes the slow growth of an economy at the same time prices are rising.

An example of this involved the **Organization of Petroleum Exporting Countries** (OPEC). They decided to increase the price of petroleum exports by 10 times. This happened during the 1973 Arab-Israeli Yom Kippur War. Inflation climbed again in Canada. Trudeau reacted. He set up a policy on Canadian crude oil. There was one price across Canada. As a result, the Canadian price of crude oil was well below the world price.

Then Trudeau got scared. Would the United States want to buy a lot of Canada's cheaper oil? This would drain Canada's supplies. He applied an oil export tax. He also had the interprovincial pipeline extended from Sarnia, Ontario, to Montreal. He then set up a national oil company. It was Petro-Canada.

Trudeau went back to the voters a second time. He revived his Trudeaumania image. This time, he wanted Canadians to see him as a family man.

Margaret had given birth to their second son on Christmas Day 1973. His name was Alexander (Sacha). Margaret agreed to help her husband with his campaign. Since he was young, Trudeau had been a loner. He liked his privacy. He did not enjoy the country peeking in on his private life. But he wanted Canadians to see him in a different role. He wanted to be seen as a father and a husband, too.

Canadian voters liked Margaret's presence. The press enjoyed taking pictures of her. The nation loved seeing them. Trudeau could focus on politics with the attention given to his wife.

Trudeau won the election once again. He returned to Ottawa with a majority government. He got busy right away. He was ready to take on a fight with the economy. He didn't realize he had to face another battle. The second battle was on the home front.

Margaret had lots of attention during the election. She had enjoyed it. She even gave some speeches herself. The day after the votes were counted, life went back to normal. Trudeau spent most of his time away. When he was at home, he was busy working in his office.

Margaret was still very young. She didn't know what to do. She had spent seven weeks with Pierre on the election trail. They had been the best weeks in her married life. Suddenly they were over. Later, she told a writer, "Something in me broke that day." To another reporter she described what happened to her as a fantasy. "It was a fairy tale at the beginning of our marriage and our relationship. It was bliss, just bliss. But I was very young. I had a lot of growing to do. The world was not a place for fairy tales. Fairy tales don't happen. Real life happens."

The couple was so different. They had different ideas. "Culture to me," she said, "was rock music." They had trouble talking about things that interested both of them.

They were at a dinner party once. Trudeau turned to his friends and said, "Don't worry about her. She wouldn't know what we were saying, even if we were speaking English."

Trudeau expected Margaret to change to make their marriage work. Margaret couldn't. She began to argue with the household staff. She also spent lots of money. She bought expensive clothes. She did a lot of home decorating. She made new friends. She went on holidays alone and tried to forget how unhappy she was.

She wanted her husband's attention. She didn't get it. She became unhappy. It was September, just two months after the election. Margaret threatened to kill herself with a kitchen knife. That night, she was admitted to Montreal General Hospital. She was suffering from severe stress.

For Margaret, it was a break from that "large cold grey mansion" on Sussex Drive.

Chapter 8
Eating His Words

T rudeau faced two crises in his life in 1975. He could not separate home from his job. When he was on the job in Ottawa, his marriage problems bothered him. Margaret was released from the hospital. She still saw a doctor. Trudeau encouraged her to do something new. She decided to try photography. She took lessons. She wanted to become a professional.

Trudeau had never lost any real battle in his life. He was not about to lose his wife. He realized that he'd been learning about parenting and politics at the same time. He later said, "Perhaps it was a little too much for me. Regrettably, I didn't succeed all that well."

On September 2, Trudeau held Michel in his arms. Michel was his third son. Trudeau devoted himself to his family. It didn't last long. Canada needed him just as much.

Inflation had risen higher. It had leaped to a rate of 10.8 percent per year. There was danger of it going out of control. Unemployment was slightly better. But seven percent of the people who were able to work in the country were out of work. Trudeau had tried something new to help the economy. "Tripartite" had failed. This was major companies, unions, and government working together to make the economy stronger. Trudeau had to find an answer.

The economy had been an issue during the election. The Conservative leader had presented a plan to save the economy. Robert Stanfield had suggested wage and price controls would maybe be the answer. Trudeau had criticized their plan. His finance minister had also criticized this idea. John Turner was Trudeau's finance minister. Then Turner changed his mind. He felt wage and price controls were what was needed. But he had criticized them. How could he recommend them?

On September 10, Turner resigned. He said he was tired. He needed to spend more time with his family. This made things worse. The press wanted answers. What was Trudeau going to do about the problems with the economy?

Trudeau searched for someone to take Turner's place. He found Donald Macdonald. MacDonald was also against wage and price controls. Trudeau knew that. Macdonald took over as finance minister. Once he did, he realized that Canada had no choice.

On Thanksgiving Day, Trudeau went on CBC television. He made an announcement to the Canadian people. He announced the creation of the Anti-Inflation Board (AIB). The federal government would be the first to freeze spending and wages in the civil service. They would be an example for the country. Trudeau hoped business and labour would follow their example. It did. Inflation began to drop. By 1976, it slid to 7.5 percent. In 1977, it stayed at about 7.9 percent.

Many criticized Trudeau's decision. Experts said the controls hurt the economy. Some felt the controls took money away from the people and gave it to the businesses. Without the controls, this would not have happened.

Government was also spending more than it was making. This spending was digging Canada deeper into debt. In 1975, the **national deficit** was $3.8 billion. It was thought to become $10.9 billion by 1978. Trudeau did not make a big deal out of this. He felt things were getting better with Canada's economy. Next, he had to deal with the matter of uniting Canada.

The prime minister was pleased with the news from Quebec. Rene Lévesque wanted separatism for Quebec. In 1970, his idea was supported by just 23 percent of the popular vote. In 1973, he tried again. This time, there was a bit more support. Thirty percent of the popular vote supported his idea of separatism. Trudeau hoped separatism was dead in Quebec.

Trudeau believed he had to heal the wounds of separatism. He would do that by renewing the **Constitution of Canada**. He knew Quebec's support was impossible. The separatist party was in politics to break up Canada. They weren't there to save it.

He knew it was also a dream to have all of Canada's premiers agree. Each province had demands of its own. This list of demands grew each time the premiers sat down together.

Trudeau had his own dream of Canada. He wanted the country to have its own Constitution. But he couldn't get the provinces to agree. He would have to do something different. The federal government would have to ask London to release their power over Canada without consent from all the provinces.

His efforts to agree with his wife at home were no better. Over the next three years, his marriage continued to fail. Finally, in March 1977, he and Margaret made a decision. They would separate. The boys would stay with him. Margaret would explore a new life apart from him. Her new life interested the media. They watched as she danced the night away in nightclubs. They followed her to backstage parties with rock musicians.

Trudeau felt battered. His wife's adventures were in the news all the time. His leadership was criticized in every part of the country. In 1978, his popularity was at an all-time low in the west. Canadian oil prices had been raised to world levels. The federal government had reached an agreement with Alberta. The province would share their resources with the rest of Canada.

Then the roof caved in on oil prices a second time. Mohammed Rez Pahlavi was thrown out of power in Iran. Pahlavi had been the Shah. Iran stopped producing oil. Overnight, the world price shot up. It went from $14 to over $34 a barrel. It was predicted that the price of oil could climb to as much as $100 a barrel.

Trudeau was alarmed. These prices would hurt Canadians. Canada could no longer rely on oil from countries like Iran. They were too unstable. They would have to rely on Alberta's oil.

In October 1980, the Liberals announced the National Energy Program (NEP). This program would share Alberta's wealth. It would encourage Canadian ownership of the energy industry. It would promote lower prices. These changes would help Canada as a whole.

Oil had provided over half the Alberta budget since the late 1960s. The OPEC price hikes had created huge profits in Alberta. Trudeau felt all Canadians should share those profits.

With the NEP, Ottawa introduced new taxes. These taxes would give the Canadian government money from the sale of Alberta's oil. Trudeau called for 50 percent Canadian ownership in the oil and gas sector.

Peter Lougheed was the premier of Alberta. He was furious. "The Ottawa government — without negotiation and without agreement — simply walked into our homes and occupied the living room."

Trudeau wanted to keep Canadian oil prices below world prices. Eastern Canada needed cheaper oil to run their industries. The NEP caused panic in the oil industry. American and foreign companies took their money out. Alberta's oil and gas exploration needed their money to survive. Businesses closed. Jobs were lost. Albertans also began calling for separation.

Alberta reacted. The province decided to sell less oil to the rest of Canada. This forced Ottawa to buy more expensive oil from other countries. This is not what Trudeau wanted.

Trudeau's team bargained with Alberta right away. In September 1981, a compromise was reached. But it would not change things. In Alberta, people were out of work. There was no more work to find. Albertans were losing their homes.

Trudeau did not apologize for trying to share resources with all Canadians. He believed a good leader was strong. He stuck by his main beliefs.

* * *

Trudeau had not done much about **foreign policy**. He felt it was time to change that. He made visits to all the major nations of the world. He got Canada accepted into the **Group of Seven**. He offered more of Canada's money to help countries that needed it. Then he called for another election in the coming March.

His wife Margaret was flying back and forth across the Atlantic Ocean. She did this a lot. When she was home, she fought with Trudeau over money. She liked to talk about her new lifestyle. She had taken small acting parts in low-budget movies. These movies were shot in Montreal and the south of France. She had tried taking pictures for *People* magazine.

Trudeau had grown tired. There was too much tension at home and in Parliament. He talked to Margaret. He wanted to try to save their marriage. He even made a promise. He would leave politics and Ottawa if that would help the marriage. At first Margaret agreed. By the end of the year, she no longer wanted to stay. To Margaret, the marriage had no future.

Margaret gave interviews. She talked about the problems in their marriage. She also decided to tell her own story in book form. Caroline Moorehead was a ghostwriter. She helped Margaret write her book, *Beyond Reason*. It came out at the beginning of Trudeau's next election campaign.

The book did not help Trudeau's campaign. The opposition government used it against the Liberals. They said the Liberals were tired. They couldn't do the job, and they had no values. The Conservatives won the election.

Trudeau faced his party after the election. He made a brave promise. His government would rise again to fight another day. The day after the election, his promise was almost lost. There were pictures of Margaret in the newspaper. She had been dancing the night away in New York's Studio 54 nightclub. They were taken on the same night Trudeau had lost the election.

Trudeau moved his boys from 24 Sussex Drive. The boys were aged eight, six, and four. Then he went on a long canoe trip in the Northwest Territories. He paddled all day for an entire week. He canoed with men half his age. He let his beard grow. He took a trip to Tibet and China. He began dating again. This time, it was with Liona Boyd. She is a classical guitarist. He also spent time with his boys. He took his sons to western Canada. They toured the national parks.

Fall came. Trudeau had to return to Ottawa. He began to think about retiring from politics. He wanted to spend more time with his family. He also knew people wanted him to leave. He had not won the election.

Trudeau had become more quiet and sad. "I could imagine someone else being prime minister," he wrote. "I couldn't imagine anyone else being the father of my children."

He thought he had made his decision. He was at a Liberal Party convention in Toronto in November 1979. He had visited a friend in the Beaches area of the city. He decided to walk back to his downtown hotel. He walked alone along the beach. He tried to make up his mind. He knew he had to decide soon. Was he going to leave or not? He liked the idea of walking on the beach as a free man.

He decided he would resign. Joe Clark was the new prime minister. Trudeau thought Clark would only be in power for a short time. Soon, a new election would be called. He wanted to give his own party enough time to choose a new leader. They had to have a new leader before it was time for a new election. He was right. Joe Clark was forced to call an election.

Clark was slow to organize his government. The Conservative party was new to power. They still had lots to learn. Clark could have waited to announce his budget. However, he wanted to show Canadians that his party was ready to run the country. John Crosbie presented a budget. He was Clark's finance minister. The budget announced a four-cent per litre hike in the gasoline tax.

Parliament was called together on December 13. Trudeau had been counting chairs and smiling. Joe Clark should have made sure of one thing. He should have made sure he had enough of his government present to vote. That would guarantee support of his new budget. But he didn't. Many of the Conservative MPs weren't there. They were still busy doing their jobs elsewhere in Canada. They were not in the House to vote for Crosbie's budget that day.

Trudeau got busy. He contacted the Liberals. He told them to get to Ottawa to vote. Their effort was tremendous. They hired private planes. They drove through the night. One MP was even rushed from the hospital in an ambulance. Then the time came to vote on Crosbie's budget. The Conservative government lost to the Liberals — 133 to 139.

Joe Clark had to call an election right away. He set the date for February 18, 1980. He hoped that Canadians would vote him back in.

The Liberals had to make a decision. Was Pierre Trudeau still their leader? Would he be the best one to lead their party into the election? Many saw Trudeau's marriage as an election problem. Margaret's lifestyle was still hot news.

In its September issue, one magazine had published an interview with her. In it, Margaret told all. She told about her love affairs with famous men. She also told about having an abortion as a teen. Another magazine had published wild photos of Margaret in a New York nightclub.

How would the Canadian public see a man with a failed marriage? Would they see him as capable of running the country? His wife and the things she did often hit the news more than the prime minister.

Pierre knew what was being said behind his back. When he was asked if he still planned on being the Liberal leader, he gave a curious answer. He told a story.

It was about a former prime minister in China. This prime minister was asked by the emperor to return. "I've had enough of it," Pierre said. "I will come back only if the emperor asks three times on bended knee." Then he left. He was angry at the things said against Margaret and his marriage.

The Liberals argued for a while. But they did ask three times. First, the caucus begged him to come back. Then the executive of the party asked him. Lastly, it was Gérard Pelletier. At the same time, Marc Lalonde and Jean Marchand told him not to return. They were Trudeau's friends. Trudeau wasn't sure.

He took a long walk. He decided not to return as leader. By morning, he had changed his mind. René Lévesque had come to power for another term in Quebec. If Trudeau left government, he could no longer fight separatism. He was 60 years old. He wanted the chance to slay the separatist dragon once and for all.

It was the morning of December 18. Trudeau called his closest advisors and gave them the news. He would run for another election.

Margaret's book had told everything about their tragic marriage. It shocked the nation. Many Canadians felt pity for Margaret after reading the book.

Life was no happier for Margaret after her book was published. Money was a problem. She was not doing well as a photographer. Her book publisher had gone out of business. It did not pay her. And Pierre was not generous with money.

Trudeau had taken his boys to Montreal to see an amazing house. A French-Canadian architect had built it. His name was Ernest Cormier. Trudeau had bought it, furniture and all. He thought he was going to retire. Margaret was also in Montreal. She was going to drive back to Ottawa with Trudeau and the boys.

The night before they left, they tucked the boys into bed. Margaret and Trudeau began to discuss money. Trudeau had to go on the campaign trail. The boys would be staying with her during that time. She asked if he would help her out with some extra money.

Trudeau smiled. "Of course," he said. He tugged his wallet from his jacket. "Will $50 do?"

His answer angered Margaret. She erupted in a white-hot fury. She screamed and attacked Trudeau. In the tussle that followed, he tried to hold her down. He shouted orders for her to stay calm. Their angry voices awoke the children. Sadly, Sasha and Michel saw their fight. Trudeau spent a half-hour talking to four-year-old Michel. Michel was very upset. Then Trudeau left. That night marked the end of their marriage.

Chapter 9
Welcome to the 80s

Trudeau was on the election trail again. His campaign team noticed a difference in "the boss." He was more mellow. He had less fits of temper. Was it because he had failed at something important to him? Was it because his marriage had failed?

He faced Conservative Joe Clark. Clark was letting U.S. oil companies take control in Canada. Trudeau didn't like what Clark was doing. Trudeau wanted Canada to control the energy industry. Under Trudeau's glare, Clark came across as well meaning but weak. The media called him "Joe Who?"

Then, there was the separatism question in Quebec. Clark told Canadians how he saw Canada. He thought Canada was a "community of communities." He didn't see it as a federation. That made Trudeau angry. Trudeau argued loudly that Canada was greater than that. Canada saw how much he believed in what he was saying.

Businesses hated Trudeau. Unions still hated Trudeau. They hadn't forgotten the wage-and-price control program of 1975. But Canada responded to his message. They sent the Liberals back to Ottawa. This time, they returned with a majority government. Trudeau was at the Château Laurier after the win. He took to the stage. He was smiling broadly. He said, "Welcome to the 1980s!"

For his next term as prime minister, he would focus on four things. He would focus on Quebec's referendum. The energy issue and the economy would be key areas. He would also focus on the Constitution. He made another decision just for himself. He would live every day as though it was his last.

He tried to become partners with the New Democratic Party (NDP). Ed Broadbent turned him down. Broadbent was the NDP leader.

Rene Lévesque was still at work in Quebec. He wanted the people of Quebec to agree to separatism. Trudeau decided to step forward. He spoke out about separatism. His argument was simple.

"They are asking you to say yes to a question that you can't honestly answer," he told French Canadians. "They are asking you whether you want an association with the other provinces. How can your vote in Quebec force the other provinces to want to associate with you if you separate?"

Her Majesty Queen Elizabeth II, with Prime Minister
Pierre Trudeau, signs the Constitution on April 17, 1982.

It was a good argument for Quebecers to hear. The
rest of Canada would not support association with an
independent Quebec.

Lévesque responded with emotion. He suggested
that someone with an English name could not be a true
Quebecer. He said, "His name is Pierre Elliott Trudeau.
This is the Elliott side taking over, and that's the English
side. We French Canadians in Quebec can't expect any
sympathy from him."

Many Quebecers had not yet made up their
mind. With that comment, they turned away from
separatism.

Trudeau made a promise to the Quebec people. A
"No" vote would mean change. If they did not agree to
separate, he would change things for them. He pledged

to bring home a new Constitution. It would have a charter of rights and a formula to make changes. The people of Quebec cast their votes in the referendum. The votes were counted. The "no" side had 59.6 percent of the votes. The prime minister wasted no time.

The next morning, Trudeau called Jean Chrétien. He asked Chrétien to begin selling the new Constitution package to the province. Chrétien did his best. Quebec wouldn't buy his sales pitch. Quebec refused to sign the Constitutional Accord.

The other provinces demanded more and more rights. Trudeau didn't think he would ever get them to agree. He tried something different.

He went straight to Great Britain. He went without the support of the provinces. On October 2, 1980, Trudeau faced the nation on TV. He told Canadians about his talks with Great Britain's Parliament. The discussions had been a success. The Constitution would finally come home to Canada.

The Constitution Act of 1982 was proclaimed on April 17. Queen Elizabeth II arrived that day. She signed it into law. The Constitution was home. So was the Charter of Rights and Freedoms. Trudeau cut Canada's last ties with Britain. No longer would Britain hold the power to make laws for Canada. No longer would Canada have to ask Britain to make any changes to their laws. Canada was now in charge of making and changing its own laws.

Chapter 10
The Statesman Departs

T rudeau had finished almost everything he had
set out to do. The Constitution and the Charter of
Rights and Freedoms had come home to Canada.
He was pleased with that. There was one more thing he
needed to do. This was a more global concern. Trudeau
wanted to decrease the making of nuclear weapons.

He called for a stop to all development of weapons.
He asked the world to cut down its supply of nuclear
weapons. Canada was the first country that chose not to
build nuclear weapons. He made sure diplomats from
around the world knew that. Canada was also the first
country to get rid of nuclear arms. He took pride in that.

Canada was part of the North Atlantic Treaty
Organization (NATO). His NATO partners did not like
his plan for peace. NATO had a commitment. It had

to match the number of guns made in the central and eastern European communist states. The Soviets had introduced a powerful new SS-20 missile. NATO wanted to threaten them back. The United States had designed new cruise missiles. Those missiles were their threat. First, they needed to be tested.

Canada was a member of NORAD. Trudeau had to allow cruise missile testing over Canadian soil. This was the man who wanted the making of weapons to stop. Having to allow the testing made him look like he didn't mean it. It also made him focus even more on the threats of nuclear war.

It was the summer of 1983. Trudeau decided it was time to move forward. He had a peace plan for the world. It might end the **Cold War**. His plan had five ways Canada might help to get East and West talking peace:

- There should be more talks on getting rid of nuclear weapons.
- A stronger agreement not to create more weapons was needed.
- There should be fewer armed forces in Europe.
- There should be a five-power disarmament conference.
- High-altitude testing of anti-satellite missiles should be banned.

The world did not accept his ideas. Trudeau met all the leaders. From his efforts, they did begin to talk. They decided to make a global effort to limit nuclear arms.

On February 9, 1984, Trudeau made a report to the House of Commons. He told them that Canadians saw a crisis and acted. Canadians took risks. Canada talked with the friendly countries. They also talked with those less willing to talk. Because of those talks, Canada lifted the shadow of war.

After all this travel, Trudeau began to think about his future. It was not long after his speech to the House of Commons. He decided to go for a walk. He walked in a raging Ottawa blizzard. He and Margaret got divorced that year. Soon after, Margaret married Fred Kemper. He was an Ottawa real-estate developer. Later, they would have two more children.

"My three boys were entering their teens. I felt the need to spend more time with them," Trudeau recalled. "For all their lives until then, from the moment each of them was born, they had been the prime minister's children. They had been set apart from others by that fact. They had been accompanied by bodyguards and so on. I wanted them to spend at least their teenage years as ordinary youngsters in Montreal, entirely away from public life. I also didn't know whether I had the energy left to fight another gruelling election campaign."

The next day, he retired. Pierre moved his boys to Montreal. He moved out of the public eye. He took time to scuba dive and canoe. He treated his boys to trips. They went to France, Ireland, and Scotland. They also travelled to China and Southeast Asia. Trudeau was

65 and eager to keep working. He accepted a job in a law firm.

Trudeau stayed out of the public until October 1995. Sometimes he gave an interview. At 76 years old, he came forward again. There was to be another separatist referendum in his province. He argued against it. The referendum failed. But, the "no" side won only by a 0.6 percent majority.

Trudeau began to make the news again. This time, it was for personal reasons. On May 5, 1991, it was made known that Trudeau had fathered a daughter. Her name was Sarah. Her mother was Deborah Coyne. She was a Liberal Party constitutional lawyer. Coyne was 36. He was 71. It was a secret Trudeau had kept closely.

There was a tragic accident seven years later. On November 13, 1998, Michel died at 23 years of age. He was Pierre and Margaret's youngest son. An avalanche swept him to the bottom of Kokanee Lake in British Columbia. The entire country reached out with their hearts to Pierre and Margaret. Michel was like his father. He was an adventure lover. Trudeau's friends said he never recovered from the loss.

Neither did Margaret. "I miss him every day, but I understand that death is part of life," she told a newspaper. "I've survived the worst of it. Such horror no one can survive without faith." Margaret and her second husband split up soon after Michel's death. Margaret later became active with WaterCan. WaterCan is an

Ottawa-based organization. It works to provide clean drinking water in developing countries. She also began working with the Canadian Avalanche Association. She promoted avalanche awareness.

In a way, Michel's death created a bond between his parents. Margaret and Pierre met often after Michel was gone. They discussed their children. In the end, they built a close friendship. It went beyond the pain of their divorce.

On September 7, 2000, Canada learned that Pierre Elliott Trudeau was dying. He was as much a symbol of Canada as the maple leaf. He had been named "Canada's newsmaker of the century." Roses were piled at his doorstep. They had been the symbol of his sauciness for many years. Canadians across the country shared their memories.

Some continued to hate him. They didn't hide their feelings. They criticized him for a huge national debt. They said Canada could never repay it. Albertans hadn't forgotten his NEP disaster. Others remembered that when he thought of Canada, he mostly saw Ottawa, Montreal, and Toronto.

Some Canadians were kinder. They may not have agreed with his vision. Even so, they respected his intellect. He was a poet, they said. He spoke to the hearts of a nation.

The opinions were as varied as Canada. For the most part, Canadians prepared themselves for his death.

They got ready to grieve the loss of their most outstanding native son. Everyone could agree on one thing. He had truly changed their country.

A note was given to the press in the late afternoon the day after his death. Justin and Sacha Trudeau told the nation that their father had passed away the day before. He died shortly after 3 p.m. on September 28, 2000. He had Parkinson's disease and prostate cancer.

More than 13,000 people filed past Trudeau's casket. He lay in state at Montreal City Hall. The line-up was three hours long. In Ottawa, more than 60,000 paid their respects. The Canadian media reported his funeral with sympathy.

Newspapers and television reporters offered time and space for Canadians to remember *their* prime minister. People shared their personal stories of Pierre Trudeau. In Canada, it marked an ending moment in our history.

The grand church in the heart of Old Montreal was filled with politicians. Close friends and family crowded the church. Canada felt a part of that ceremony. Canadians crowded around television sets wherever they were. Some watched in sports bars and shopping malls. Others watched in school auditoriums and living rooms. They watched in silence. Cuban President Fidel Castro hugged the boys. Former U.S. president Jimmy Carter embraced nine-year-old Sarah. As Canadians watched, they wept.

Across the nation, tributes were made. Church bells tolled. Office work stopped. Everywhere, workers observed a moment of silence. In that moment, they remembered their gunslinger prime minister. There was an outpouring of grief. Justin Trudeau quietly gave his father's eulogy. Canada listened in a hush that was 5,000 kilometres wide.

The young man talked about his dad. He talked about his playful side. He gave a glimpse of his father's character as well.

Justin spoke of a day his father taught him the meaning of respect. The two were sharing a meal in a restaurant. Justin was just eight years old at the time. He recognized one of his father's political rivals seated nearby. He wanted to please his father so he told a joke. It was nothing great. It was just a silly grade school joke. His father looked at him sternly. He said, "Justin, never attack the individual." Trudeau told his son that he could disagree with someone. However, he should never put that person down.

Saying that, he stood up and took Justin by the hand. He took him over to the table where his rival was eating with his daughter. He introduced Justin to this man. The man spoke to Justin in a friendly manner. It was then that Justin understood something. You can have a different opinion from someone else. But you should hold that person in the highest regard.

Trudeau had taught his son an important lesson.

Tolerance was not enough. Each person had to have true and deep respect for every human being. It didn't matter if people differed in their beliefs, origins, and values. Trudeau demanded that respect of his sons. He also expected it of his country.

Canadians lined the route on Trudeau's final journey. His flag-draped coffin was carried in state on train number 638. As it passed through stations, people reached out to touch the black-curtained car that carried his coffin. They sang "O Canada" in both English and French.

Pierre Elliott Trudeau was buried next to his mother. Only family attended the private ceremony.

Epilogue

Trudeau was a great Canadian. His life is a story of amazing achievements. It is also one of significant failures. Trudeau changed Canada's divorce law. He introduced official bilingualism. He created a ministry to protect our environment. His tax policies forced Canadians to think about their future retirement. He brought the Constitution to Canada. This cut Canada's ties to Great Britain. He also established a Charter of Rights and Freedoms. These rights and freedoms are important for all Canadians.

He put wage and price control into effect. He created debt. His National Energy Program angered westerners. He often cared too little about the problems of prairie farmers or east coast fishermen.

Sometimes he showed his anger with a curse. Other times, he showed compassion with a prayer. When all is considered, he was a man of true greatness.

He had a vision of a better world. Canadians felt the power of his intellect. They also felt his passion and will. Pierre Elliott Trudeau showed us what it means to be a Canadian.

Glossary

Apprehended insurrection: A perceived revolt against the government.

Autonomy: Independence; a self-governing community.

British North America Act: On July 1, 1867, the British parliament passed the BNA Act. This law established the Dominion of Canada. It gave the Canadian government the right to pass the laws. However, Canada still needed the approval of the British parliament.

Caucus: A meeting of the MPs of one party to discuss policies, plan strategy, etc.

Civil servant: An employee who works for a government department.

Cold War: The stand-off between the superpowers of the former Soviet Union and the United States, supported by their alliance partners. It lasted from about 1947 to the fall of the Berlin Wall on November 11, 1989.

Conscription: When government forces its citizens to serve in the armed forces.

Constitution of Canada: The supreme law in Canada. It outlines Canada's system of government, as well as the civil rights of all Canadian citizens.

Economics: A social science that deals with the production, distribution, and consumption of goods and services.

Federalism: A method of political organization in which two levels of government have power. One level governs the country as a whole, the other governs the provinces.

Foreign policy: A set of political goals which seek to outline how a country will cooperate with the other countries of the world. Creating foreign policy is usually the job of the head of government and the foreign minister.

Front de libération du Québec (Quebec Liberation Front): Also known as the FLQ, this was a terrorist group in Canada founded in 1963. Its goal was to achieve Quebec independence.

Group of Seven: The members of the Group of Seven (G-7) are Canada, France, Germany, Italy, Japan, the United Kingdom, and the United States. The leaders of these rich nations have met annually since 1975 to discuss major economic and political issues.

Inflation: A sharp and sudden rise of prices as a result of too great an increase in the supply of money or credit.

National deficit: When a country spends more money than it takes in.

Nationalism: The desire of a people to preserve its own language, religion, and traditions. In Canada, some of the people of Quebec believed Quebec needed to either form its own country or have more control in the government of Canada.

Martial law: A system of rules that takes effect (usually after a formal declaration) when a military authority takes control of a country. Martial law usually reduces the personal rights of citizens.

Organization of Petroleum Exporting Countries (OPEC): A group of 11 nations who rely on the money made by producing and exporting oil. One of OPEC's jobs is to regulate oil prices in a way that is fair to both producers and consumers.

Parti Québécois: A political party founded in 1968. It promotes Quebec independence.

War Measures Act: A special law that grants extra powers to the government and police in times of emergency. In Canada, the War Measures Act has been used three times: WWI, WWII, and the October Crisis.

About the Author

Stan Sauerwein lives and writes in Westbank, BC. A freelance writer for two decades, Stan has published articles in a variety of Canadian and U.S. magazines and newspapers. Specializing in business subjects, he has written for both corporations and governments. He has written several Amazing Stories including: *Gentleman Train Robber, Klondike Joe Boyle, Lucy Maud Montgomery, Ma Murray, Moe Norman, Rattenbury,* and *Soapy Smith.*

Photo Credits

Cover: D. Cameron/National Archives of Canada (PA-111213); D. Cameron/National Archives of Canada: page 63 (PA-143959), 83 (PA-141503).